THE BLUE-COLLAR POET

BY

PAUL E. GRAY

THE BLUE-COLLAR POET

BY
PAUL E. GRAY

ISBN- 978-1-965408-12-4

PUBLISHED BY

BOOK WRITING LEAGUE

THIS IS MY LEGACY

IT TELLS THE WORLD I WAS HERE

PAUL E. GRAY

THE BLUE-COLLAR POET

TO MY WIFE, STEPHANIE
FROM YOUR HUSBAND,
PAUL E. GRAY
THE BLUE-COLLAR POET

DEDICATED TO SNIGGLES

TO MY WIFE STEPHANIE,
FOR WITHOUT YOU, I AM NOTHING,
YOU GAVE LIFE, HOPE, AND DREAMS,
I HOPE I ALWAYS MAKE YOU PROUD.
MY LOVE YOU
UGLY

I DEDICATE MY POEMS TO MY WIFE, STEPHANIE

MY DREAM COME TRUE
SHE WAS MY BEST FRIEND
SHE BELIEVED IN ME
THANK YOU WEETIES!!!

ALL MY LOVE UGLY
2023 PAUL E. GRAY
THE BLUE-COLLAR POET

FOREWORD

PLEASE BEAR WITH MY WRITING,
FOR THE SPELLING IS VERY BAD,
I AM LACKING THE EDUCATION,
THAT NOW I WISH I HAD!!!

AUNT TERESA WROTE THIS TO ME

YOUR POETRY IS EXCEPTIONALLY FINE.
MUCH DIFFERENT FROM MINE,
TIS NOT TO BE SCATTERED ABOUT
YOURS SHOULD BE WRITTEN DOWN
AND NOT CAUSE ME TO FROWN
SO PLEASE USE THIS LITTLE BOOK
AND YOU'LL NOT HAVE TO LOOK AND LOOK
FOR THOSE PAPERS WRINKLED AND OLD AND WITH MANY A FOLD
NOW, IN ONE PLACE, THEY WILL BE,
AND WE CAN ALL OF THEM SEE
HAPPY BIRTHDAY
AUNT TERESA

MY REPLY TO AUNT THERESA

THANK YOU FOR THIS BOOK
TODAY I RECEIVED A PRESENT
DECIDED TO TAKE A LOOK
EAGERLY REMOVED THE WRAPPING
WHAT A SURPRISE, A POETRY BOOK,
SOMETHING I SURELY NEEDED
TO KEEP MYY THOUGHTS SO NEAT
FROM A THOUGHTFUL, LOVING PERSON
WHO IS KIND AND ALSO SWEET
I HOPE TO DO IT JUSTICE
WITH VERSEs THAT COMES TO MIND
AND HOPE SOMEDAY TO SHARE IT
WITH THE WORLD AND ALL MANKIND

Table of Contents

A DAY
IN THE LIFE OF
PAUL E. GRAY

BEAUTIFUL

SHE WAS KNOWN AS BEAUTIFUL
I, AS UGA BUNS
NOW THAT SHE'S NOT HERE
MY LIFE IS NOT MUCH FUN

MY DAY'S ARE FILLED WITH SADNESS
SOMEHOW IT DOESN'T SEEM FAIR
MY DAILY ROUTINE IS EMPTY
NO ONE SEEMS TO CARE

THE WORLD IS A LONELY PLACE
WHEN YOU LOSE THE ONE YOU LOVE
YOU LOOK TOWARDS THE HEAVENS
FOR HELP FROM UP ABOVE

YOU TRY TO GET THROUGH
EVERY SINGLE DAY
NO ONE TO TALK TO
YOU HAVE NOTHING TO SAY

IT'S LEFT UP TO FATE
WHAT YOUR LIFE WILL UNFOLD
YOU PRAY TO THE HEAVENS
FOR SOMEONE TO HOLD

NOT KNOWING THE FUTURE
CAN BRING YOU MUCH PAIN
YOU HOPE TO FIND SOMEONE
AND NOT GO INSANE

I'VE BEEN LUCKY IN LOVE
NOW I'M ALONE

Paul E Gray

NO ONE TO TALK TO
NO ONE TO COME HOME

I SPEND MY LIFE
WITH NOTHING TO DO
I WANDER HOPELESSLY
JUST LOOKING FOR YOU

I KNOW YOU WON'T COME
IT'S LIKE LIVING IN HELL
THERE'S NOTHING I CAN DO
I SIMPLY GO INTO A SPELL

I'LL TRY TO CONTINUE
WITH MY EVERYDAY LIFE
TRYING TO COPE
WITHOUT MY BEAUTIFUL WIFE

BEAUTIFUL

P.S.

I COULD NOT REMEMBER MY OLD POEM
SO I HAD TO WRITE A NEW ONE
I HOPE TO DO IT JUSTICE
I HOPE IT MAKES SOME SENSE
I HOPE YOU ENJOY IT

Paul E Gray

BUTTERFLY

BUTTERFLY UPON THE WALL,
ARE YOU THE FREE-EST OF THEM ALL,
IF YOU ARE, PLEASE SHOW ME THE WAY,
BECAUSE I CAN'T STAND ANOTHER DAY.

SPREAD YOUR WINGS, TAKE TO YOUR FLIGHT,
THE FREEDOM YOU KNOW MAKES THE WORLD SEEM RIGHT,
TRY TO RELATE YOUR FEELINGS TO ME,
LET ME USE YOUR EYES TO SEE.

I WISH I HAD THE POWER TO SOAR AND FLY,
I WISH I HAD THE CHANCE TO CARESS THE SKY,
TO ABSORB THE THINGS THAT ARE DEAR TO ME,
TO FIND OUT WHAT IT'S LIKE TO REALLY BE FREE.

IT MUST BE NICE TO FLOW WITH THE BREEZE,
IT MUST BE NICE TO GLIDE THROUGH THE TREES,
IF I COULD ONLY FIND A WAY,
I WOULD LIKE TO TAKE YOUR PLACE TODAY

SCHOOLHOUSE

I AM A ONE ROOM SCHOOLHOUSE,
THAT HAS STOOD FOR A HUNDRED YEARS,
ONCE I WAS FILLED WITH CHILDREN,
WHO WERE INFLUENCED BY THEIR PEERS.

I RECALL THE CHILDREN'S HAPPINESS,
THEIR EAGERNESS TO LEARN,
A WELL-ROUNDED EDUCATION,
WAS THE PARENT'S TRUE CONCERN.

I STILL REMEMBER THE LAUGHTER,
THE EYES AND SMILES SO BRIGHT,
THE FEELINGS OF THE SADNESS,
WHEN THEY LOCKED MY DOORS FOR THE NIGHT.

THE MEMORIES OF THE BLACKBOARD,
WHERE THE TEACHER KEPT HER NAME,
THE SCREAMING OF THE CHALK,
AND THE EARS THAT WINCED IN PAIN.

I REMEMBER THE CHILDREN'S DESKS,
THE TEACHER'S DESK AS WELL,
THE BUSINESS OF THE BULLETIN BOARD,
AND THE RINGING OF THE BELL.
I RECALL THE GLOBE OF THE WORLD,
EVEN THE PULL-DOWN MAP,
THE STOOL IN THE CORNER,
WHERE THE DUNCE SAT IN HIS CAP.

I WON'T FORGET THE HOLIDAYS,
AND THE JOYOUS MOOD AROUND,

Paul E Gray

I WAS DRESSED UP TO FIT THE OCCASION,
THE MOST DECORATED BUILDING IN TOWN.

IN THE SPRING I WAS ALWAYS SADDENED,
FOR I KNEW THAT JUNE WAS NEAR,
I HATED TO STAND EMPTY,
UNTIL FALL BEGAN A NEW YEAR.

NOW I SIT HERE DORMANT,
NO CHILDREN'S ECHOES DO I HEAR,
I TRY TO GIVE A SILENT CRY,
BUT IT FALLS ON DEAFENED EARS.

MY PURPOSE HAS BEEN ENDED,
NO NEW USEFULNESS HAS BEEN FOUND,
TOMORROW, A FORMER STUDENT,
WILL COME AND TEAR ME DOWN

M.I.A.

BILLY SMITH IS A SERVICE MAN
IN THE ARMY, NAVY, OR CORPS
HIS COUNTRY SAID IT NEEDED HIM
TO DO HIS SOUTHEAST ASIA TOUR

TO HIS LUCK OR HIS MISFORTUNE
BILLY DISAPPEARED ONE DAY
DID HE GO TO MEET HIS MAKER
OR WAS HE LEFT BEHIND TO PAY

DOES BILLY HAVE THE STRENGTH
TO SURVIVE WHAT HE'S BEEN THROUGH
PERHAPS HE FEELS BETRAYED
MAYBE SIMPLY LIED TO

THE FACES IN HIS MIND
HAVE LONG BEGUN TO FADE
THE NOTCHES THAT HE MARKS
STAND FOR YEARS INSTEAD OF DAYS

YOU CAN NOT JUST DISCARD HIM
AND SAY THAT LIFE IS CHEAP
BILLY HAS GIVEN THE ULTIMATE
SO EVERYONE COULD REAP
NOR IS HE JUST A CASUALTY
A CASUALTY OF WAR
HE'S THERE FOR RUTH AND JUSTICE
WHAT HIS COUNTRY SHOULD STAND FOR

DID ANYONE ATTEMPT TO FIND HIM
AND GIVE IT AN EARNEST TRY

OR DID THEY MARK HIM MISSING
DEAD OR LEFT TO DIE

CAN YOU IMAGINE THE HORROR
THAT POOR BILLY HAS GONE THROUGH
DECAYING IN THE JUNGLE
ALIVE OR DEAD, FORGOT BY YOU

IF BILLY IS STILL ALIVE
OH, WHAT A SHAME
IF BILLY IS STILL ALIVE
HE CAN POINT THE BLAME

The Blue Collar Poet

FOR SOMEONE HAS TO ANSWER,
FOR THE WRONG THAT HAS BEEN DONE,
BILLY IS A TRUE HERO,
OF THE WAR THAT WAS NOT WON.

TO HE WHO WEARS THE HONOR,
OF DISTINGUISHED M.I.A.
IS YOUR MISSION OVER?
ARE YOU COMING HOME TODAY?

Paul E Gray

SURPRISE

THE ATMOSPHERE SEEMED SO PLEASANT,
BEAUTIFUL COLORS OF DIFFERENT SHADES,
I PASSED A CROWD OF HAPPY PEOPLE,
GIVING SMILES AND FRIENDLY WAVES.

THE DAY WAS GOING MAGNIFICENTLY,
AS THOUGH I HAD IT PLANNED,
TICKING TOGETHER LIKE A FINE SWISS CLOCK,
IN THE DISTANCE, I HEARD A BAND.

SUDDENLY SOMETHING FROM THE SHADOWS,
SEEMED TO HOVER OVER MY HEAD,
IT HAD SUCH A HORRIBLE FACE,
LIKE A MONSTER FROM THE DEAD.

MY BODY STARTED TO TREMBLE,
MY MIND COULDN'T UNDERSTAND WHY,
THIS GREAT, HORRENDOUS, UGLY THING,
COULD LEAVE THE GROUND AND FLY.

I STARTED TO RUN AS FAST AS I COULD,
BUT MUCH TO MY DESPAIR,
I FOUND I WAS IN THE EXACT SAME SPOT,
I HADN'T GOTTEN ANYWHERE.
HIS TEETH WERE LONG AND JAGGED,
HIS EYES WERE STOLEN FROM A CAT,
HIS BODY WAS GREEN AND SCALY,
HE FLEW WITH THE WINGS OF A BAT.

HIS HUGE HANDS BEGAN TO CLAW AT ME,
AND TEAR ABOUT MY CLOTHES,

THEN I FELT THE PAIN IN MY FACE,
AND THE WARMTH RUNNING FROM MY NOSE.

THE BLOOD WAS RUNNING ACROSS MY LIPS,
AND THEN ONTO MY TONGUE,
I WISH I KNEW THE REASON,
WHY I HAD TO BE THE ONE.

HIS FINGERS FELT LIKE RAZORS,
AS HE STARTED TO RAKE MY CHEST,
I FELT MY BODY ARCH IN FEAR,
AND SMELLED MY RAW, OOZING FLESH.

HIS BREATH WAS HOT AND STEAMY,
OH, WHATA GOD-FORSAKEN SMELL!
I KNEW HE WASN'T FROM MY WORLD,
HE MUST HAVE BEEN FROM HELL!

THERE IS NOWHERE LEFT FOR ME TO TURN,
WHAT ELSE AM I TO DO?
I FOUGHT HIM OFF THE BEST I COULD,
NOW, I GUESS I'M DOOMED.

LIFE WAS SLOWLY LEAVING,
THIS JUST DID NOT SEEM FAIR,
BUT WHAT A SURPRISE TO OPEN MY EYES,
TO END THIS HORRID NIGHTMARE!

Paul E Gray

SLEEP

WHEN I GO TO SLEEP,
I HOPE I WON'T WAKE UP.
THEN COMES THE MORNING,
NO SUCH LUCK.

LIFE IS SO PRECIOUS,
TO SOME, THAT IS TRUE.
BUT I AM ALL ALONE,
WITH NOTHING TO DO.

MY DAYS ARE CONFUSING,
CAN'T REMEMBER A THING.
I HAVE TO WRITE NOTES,
FORGET WHAT THEY MEAN.

I AM JUST GETTING OLDER,
AS YOU CAN PROBABLY TELL.
MY MEMORY IS GONE,
CAN'T WALK VERY WELL.

I GO THROUGH THE DAY,
NOT FEELING SO STRONG.
DO MY DAILY ROUTINE,
AS I STUMBLE ALONG.

MY BODY IS BREAKING DOWN,
IT'S TOUGH TO GET OLD.
IN THE DAYTIME I AM HOT,
AT NIGHT I AM COLD.

THE DAY WILL COME,
WHEN I AM FEELING WEAK.

The Blue Collar Poet

I WILL GO TO BED,
AND DIE IN MY SLEEP.

Paul E Gray

IMAGE

WHEN YOU GAZE INTO A MIRROR,
WHAT DO YOU REALLY SEE,
ARE YOU LOOKING AT AN IMAGE,
OR WHAT YOU WOULD LIKE TO BE

CAN YOU SEE THE FAULTS,
THAT YOU DESPERATELY TRIED TO HIDE,
THEY'RE NOT FLOATING ON THE SURFACE,
THEY'RE KEPT DEEP DOWN INSIDE.

DO YOU LOOK INTO THE SHADOWS,
INTO THE CLOSETS OF YOUR LIFE,
ARE YOU AFRAID OF THE SECRETS,
THAT WILL CUT YOU LIKE A KNIFE

DO YOU HAVE THE COURAGE,
TO ACCEPT WHAT YOU DO NOT LIKE,
TO CHANGE YOUR PERSONALITY,
AND TRY IT WITH ALL YOUR MIGHT.

CAN YOU TRY TO CHANGE THINGS,
WHEN YOU LOOK INTO THIS WELL,
OR DO YOU EVEN BOTHER,
SIMPLY GO INTO A SPELL
CAN YOU REALLY PASS JUDGMENT,
ARE YOUR EYES PROGRAMMED TO SLEEP,
DO YOU GET AN HONEST IMPRESSION,
OR DO YOU ONLY LOOK SKIN-DEEP.

CAN YOU LOOK INTO A MIRROR,
INTO THE WINDOWS OF YOUR MIND,

AND REALLY SEE THE UGLINESS,
THAT APPEARS FROM TIME TO TIME.

CAN YOU TRANSFORM THIS REFLECTION,
FROM THE MIRROR TO YOUR SOUL,
LIKE PANDORA'S BOX,
IT MAKES YOUR BLOOD RUN COLD.

ARE YOU PUTTING YOUR BEST FOOT FORWARD,
OR ARE YOU LISTENING TO YOUR EYES,
DO YOU REALLY SEE THE TRUTH,
OR DOES THIS IMAGE TELL YOU LIES?

Paul E Gray

BAR

A BAR, A LOUNGE,
TO ME, THEY ARE BOTH THE SAME,
FILLED WITH DIFFERENT SORTS OF PEOPLE,
WITH DIFFERENT REASONS AS TO WHY THEY CAME.

SOME ARE THERE FOR HAPPINESS,
SOME ARE THERE FOR JOY,
SOME TO MEET A GIRL,
SOME TO MEET A BOY.

AND THEY COME WITH A SMILE ON THEIR FACE,
MAYBE TO MEET SOMEONE THEY KNOW,
THEY TRIED SO HARD TO HAVE A GOOD TIME,
AND HOPE THEIR EMPTINESS DOESN'T SHOW.

SOME ARE THERE BECAUSE OF LONELINESS,
SOME BECAUSE OF NERVE,
WHICHEVER REASON PEOPLE MAY CHOOSE,
THEY WILL GET JUST WHAT THEY DESERVE.

SOME ARE THERE FOR TROUBLE,
THEY'LL LOOK AROUND FOR A FIGHT,
MARK MY WORDS, SHOULD ONE ERUPT,
IT'S OFF TO JAIL FOR THE NIGHT.
IF YOU SIT IN THE CORNER,
AND CAREFULLY LOOK AROUND,
YOU WILL SEE MANY CHARACTERS,
THE INHABITANTS OF THE TOWN.

IF YOU COULD SIT AND LISTEN,
TO THE COLORFUL STORIES THEY MAY TELL,

YOU WILL OFTEN REALIZE,
THAT THEY EACH HAVE THEIR OWN LITTLE HELL.

IF THEY WOULD ANSWER SOME QUESTIONS,
AS TO THE PURPOSE FOR WHICH THEY CAME,
MAYBE THE ONE AND ONLY REASON,
WAS PERHAPS TO EASE THE PAIN.

Paul E Gray

SHOW A LITTLE KINDNESS

SHOW A LITTLE KINDNESS,
TO THE ONE WHO'S NOT SO FAIR,
HER PLAIN AND SIMPLE FACE,
WITH HER MOUSEY DULL BROWN HAIR.

IT WAS NOT HER CHOICE TO BE THIS WAY,
FOR HER, IT'S JUST TOO LATE,
SOME WOULD SAY IT'S JUST BAD LUCK,
I GUESS YOU COULD CALL IT FATE.

HER CRITICS ARE THE PRETTY GIRLS,
WHO THINK THAT THEY'RE THINK THAT ALL THAT,
IF YOU LISTEN CLOSELY,
THEY ARE HISSING LIKE A CAT.

IF ALL WOMEN WERE BEAUTIFUL,
THEY WOULD BE LIKE A STRING OF PEARLS,
THEIR SMILES AND THEIR HAPPINESS,
WOULD BRING JOY THROUGHOUT THE WORLD.

DIFFERENT SHAPES AND DIFFERENT SIZES,
EVEN DIFFERENT COLORS TOO,
YOU HAVE NO CHOICE WHEN YOU ARE BORN,
IN FACT, YOU HAVE NO CLUE.
MANY GIRLS HAVE BEEN SPARED,
FROM THAT TERRIBLE UGLY FATE,
THEY HAVE TWO BEAUTIFUL CHILDREN,
AND A HANDSOME LOVING MATE.

SHE FEELS SO ALL ALONE,
WHEN HER FRIENDS TALK ABOUT BEING PRETTY,

The Blue Collar Poet

HER BLOOD RUNS COLD WITH ENVY,
WHAT A SHAME WHAT A PITY.

SO SHOW A LITTLE KINDNESS,
TO THE ONE WHO'S NOT SO FAIR,
FOR IF GOD SHOULD HAVE A CHANGE OF HEART,
IT COULD BE YOU THAT'S SITTING THERE

Paul E Gray

UNTITLED

I LEFT SOME BROKEN HEARTS,
ALONG THE SIDE OF THE ROAD,
SOME I WISH I KEPT,
SOME I WAS GLAD TO SEE GO.

I'M NOT MUCH TO LOOK AT,
AT LEAST IN CERTAIN WAYS,
BUT LIFE WAS VERY MUCH KINDER,
IN MY YOUTH, IN MY YOUNGER DAYS.

MY LIFE HAS BEEN SO LONELY,
BUT I DIDN'T SEEM TO CARE,
I WOULD LOVE TO HAVE SOMEONE BESIDES ME,
FOR ALL THE JOY WE COULD SHARE.

I'VE MADE SOME BAD DECISIONS,
WHEN IT CAME TO CHOOSING A MATE,
I DID NOT REALLY TRY,
I LEFT IT UP TO FATE.

I WILL TRY TO RECTIFY,
ALL THE MISTAKES I'VE MADE,
AND FIND A WONDERFUL WOMAN,
TO SHARE ALL THE LOVE I'VE SAVED.
IF I CAN'T FIND A GOOD WOMAN,
THERE'S NOTHING I CAN DO,
I'LL SET OUT TO FOLLOW MY HEART,
I GUESS I'M JUST A FOOL.

I FOUND A SPECIAL LADY,
TO SATISFY MY NEEDS,

The Blue Collar Poet

I WILL ASK HER TO MARRY ME,
ON MY BENDED KNEE.

NOW THAT I HAVE FOUND HER,
I WILL NEVER LET HER GO,
I WILL CHERISH AND LOVE HER,
WITH ALL MY HEART AND SOUL,

I FOUND A SPECIAL LADY,
TO ASK TO BE MY WIFE,
TO LOVE AND CHERISH HER,
FOR THE REST OF MY LIFE.

Paul E Gray

TRAVELER

AS I TRAVEL THROUGH MY LIFE,
NOT KNOWING WHAT TO DO,
I LET MY MIND WANDER,
THEN I THOUGHT OF YOU.

THRILLED TO HAVE YOU WITH ME,
AS I GO ALONG IN TIME,
I WISH SOME THINGS WERE DIFFERENT,
I WISH THAT YOU WERE MINE.

TO BE WITH YOU, TO HAVE FUN WITH YOU,
EVERY DAY AND EVERY NIGHT,
TO SEE YOUR FACE AND HEAR YOUR VOICE,
YOU ARE SUCH AN AWESOME SIGHT,

TO YOU, I AM SOMEONE,
WHO DOES NOT EXIST,
TO ME, YOU ARE SOMEONE,
I JUST CANNOT RESIST.

I'LL HOPE, AND I'LL PRAY,
AND TRY TO SURVIVE,
FOR MAYBE SOMEDAY,
YOU'LL NOTICE I AM ALIVE.
TO UNLEASH MY FEELINGS,
THAT I HAVE INSIDE,
TO TOUCH YOU, TO HOLD YOU,
AND BE BY YOUR SIDE.

I GUESS IT'S WISHFUL THINKING,
BUT WHAT AM I TO DO,

JUST SIT HERE AND WAIT,
FOR MY ONLY WISH TO COME TRUE

Paul E Gray

PEARL

DECEMBER 7TH 1941,
THE PLANES WERE HIDDEN BY THE SUN,
NO ONE KNOWS JUST WHY THEY'VE COME,
THEY ARE FILLED WITH DOOM AND DESTRUCTION.

TWO THOUSAND FOUR HUNDRED AND THREE PEOPLE,
DIED TODAY,
THEY HAD NO CHOICE,
THEY HAD NO SAY.

YOU CAME WHEN WE WERE SLEEPING,
AND CAUGHT US BY SURPRISE,
YOU DID NOT SEE THE RAGE,
AND THE TOUGHNESS IN OUR EYES.

NO ONE SEES THE COURAGE,
THAT LURKS INSIDE OF MEN,
IT'S TIME TO SHOW THE WORLD,
THE ANGER KEPT WITHIN.

THEY BROUGHT A FURY,
TO DESTROY OUR WORLD,
THEY BROUGHT A FURY,
TO DESTROY OUR PEARL.
THEY CAME AS A BIG SURPRISE,
TO THE MEN STATIONED THERE,
THEY WOKE A SLEEPING GIANT,
THEY DIDN'T SEEM TO CARE.

YOU WOKE A SLEEPING GIANT,
THE DAY YOU DROPPED THE BOMBS,

WE WILL FIGHT YOU TILL THE END,
FOR ALL THE LIVES WE LOST.

WE WILL GET OUR REVENGE,
FROM THE LAND OF THE RISING SUN,
WE WILL DESTROY YOU,
FOR THE DAMAGE YOU HAVE DONE.

IT'S TIME TO FEEL THE PAIN,
THAT WE HAVE INSIDE,
YOU WILL FEEL OUR MITE,
OH! WHAT A BIG SURPRISE.

THEY WOKE A SLEEPING GIANT,
DO THEY REALIZE WHAT THEY'VE DONE,
THERE WON'T BE A MINUTE'S PEACE,
TILL WE WIN THE WAR THAT YOU BEGUN.

WE WILL DEFEND OUR COUNTRY,
THE VERY BEST WE CAN,
WE WILL NOW DESTROY OUR ENEMY,
A COUNTRY KNOWN AS JAPAN.

JAPAN WILL ALWAYS REMEMBER,
THE PAIN OF A CERTAIN DAY,
THE U.S. SENT THEM A PRESENT,
DELIVERED BY ENOLA GAY.

DECEMBER 7TH 1941,
THE PLANES WERE HIDDEN BY THE SUN,
NO ONE KNOWS JUST WHY THEY'VE COME,
THEY ARE FILLED WITH DOOM AND DESTRUCTION

WIZ

WHEN YOU CLOSELY LOOK AT HIM,
THIS MAN IS A HOLLOW SHELL,
THE PAIN IS BURNING HIS INSIDES,
AS INTENSE AS THE SIRES OF HELL

TRYING TO CONTROL,
THE QUIVERING OF HIS CHIN,
LOCKING HIS EMOTIONS,
KEEPING HIS HURT WITHIN.

IT SURE IS HARD,
FOR A MAN TO REMAIN STRONG,
WHEN THE ONE HE FAITHFULLY LOVED,
IS ALL OF A SUDDEN GONE.

HIS MIND IS WILDLY RACING,
HIS THOUGHTS ARE VERY UNCLEAR,
HE WISHES HE WERE DREAMING,
AND WOULD AWAKE AND FIND HER HERE.

MINUTES SEEM LIKE HOURS,
HOURS SEEM LIKE DAYS,
HIS SOMEWHAT ROUTINE LIFE,
HAS TURNED INTO A MAZE.
HE STILL EXPECTS TO SEE HER;
HE LISTENS FOR HER VOICE,
HE CRIES HIMSELF TO SLEEP,
HE HAS NO OTHER CHOICE.

EVERYTHING IS A MEMORY,
HE CAN'T HELP BUT FEEL DEPRESSED,

Paul E Gray

AS HE PICKS UP A BOTTLE OF PERFUME,
AND STARES AT HER FAVORITE BLUE DRESS.

HER SHOES ALL LINE THE CLOSET,
HER NIGHTGOWN HANGS BY THE DOOR,
HE THINKS ABOUT LAST CHRISTMAS,
AND THE NECKLACE SHE NEVER WORE.

THE PRESSURE IS UNBEARABLE,
HE IS UNDER TREMENDOUS STRAIN,
IF HE COULD CHANGE THAT FATAL DAY,
SHE WOULD BE HOME AGAIN.

ALTHOUGH SHE IS NOT WITH HIM,
HE MUST DEAL WITH THIS TRAGIC BLOW;
HE PROMISES TO ALWAYS LOVE HER,
AS HE WAITS FOR HIS TIME TO GO.

RETREAT

THE ATMOSPHERE IS QUIET AND CHARMING,
I'VE WAITED FOR THE ESCAPE,
THE SERENITY OF THE CABIN,
IN THE MOUNTAINS, BESIDE A LAKE.

I LEFT THE CITY BEHIND ME,
WITH ITS HUSTLE, BUSTLE WAYS,
TO COME TO MY SECRET SANCTUARY,
AND ENJOY NATURE FOR A COUPLE OF DAYS.

THERE IS STILLNESS, THERE IS BEAUTY
ANIMALS MOVE WITH THEIR OWN STYLE AND GRACE,
MANY TIMES, I HAVE WONDERED,
HOW I WOULD SURVIVE WITHOUT SUCH A PLACE

TO SIT AND GAZE OUT THE WINDOW,
WATCH THE WIND BLOW THE LEAVES AROUND,
ENJOY THE WARMTH OF A FIREPLACE,
ENJOY THE PEACE I HAVE FOUND.

I MIGHT JUST DO SOME READING,
OR GET SOME WRITING DONE,
EVEN IF I JUST SIT QUIETLY,
I'M ALWAYS GLAD I'VE COME.
A WALK IN THE WOODS IS SOOTHING,
I CAN LISTEN TO THE BIRDS SING,
I EVEN GET A LITTLE ENVIOUS,
AND WISH I HAD THE USE OF THEIR WINGS.

I'VE CHERISHED MY ESCAPE FROM REALITY,
DONE SO THE ONLY WAY THAT I CAN,

Paul E Gray

TOMORROW IT'S BACK TO THE CITY,
I ALWAYS LEAVE SOONER THAN I'VE PLANNED.

THE TRIP BACK IS LESS INVIGORATING,
A RIDE I ALWAYS HATE,
IT'S NOW MONDAY MORNING.
HURRY UP, FRIDAY, BEFORE IT'S TOO LATE!

WISHFUL THINKING

AS I TRAVEL THROUGH MY LIFE
NOT KNOWING WHAT TO DO
I LET MY MIND WANDER
THEN I THOUGHT OF YOU

THRILLED TO HAVE YOU WITH ME
AS I GO ALONG IN TIME
I WISH SOME THINGS WERE DIFFERENT
I WISH THAT YOU WERE MINE

TO BE WITH YOU
HAVE FUN WITH YOU
EVERY DAY
AND EVERY NIGHT

TO SEE YOUR FACE
AND HEAR YOUR VOICE
YOU ARE SUCH
AN AWESOME SIGHT

TO YOU, I AM SOMEONE
WHO DOES NOT EXIST
TO ME, YOU ARE SOMEONE
I JUST CAN NOT RESIST
I'VE LEFT SOME BROKEN HEARTS
ALONG THE SIDE OF THE ROAD
SOME I WISH I HAD KEPT
I WAS GLAD TO SEE SOME GO

I'LL HOPE, AND I'LL PRAY
AND TRY TO SURVIVE

Paul E Gray

FOR MAYBE SOMEDAY
YOU'LL NOTICE I'M ALIVE

TO UNLEASH MY FEELINGS
THAT I HAD TO HIDE
TO TOUCH YOU TO HOLD YOU
AND BE BY YOUR SIDE

HOPES AND DREAMS

HOLD ON TO YOUR HOPES AND DREAMS
NEVER LET THEM GO
IF THEY DON'T COME TRUE TODAY
THERE WILL ALWAYS BE TOMORROW

EVERYONE HAS HOPES AND DREAMS
AND THEY WANT THEM TO COME TRUE
BUT IN TRUE REALITY
IT'S ONLY FOR A CHOSEN FEW

SOME ARE BORN UNDER LUCKY STARS
GO THROUGH LIFE WITHOUT A CARE
OTHERS HAVE TO CLAW AND FIGHT
SOMEHOW, IT DOESN'T SEEM FAIR

THINK ABOUT YOUR PAST
AND WHAT YOU HAD TO DO
WAS IT ALWAYS A STRUGGLE
OR DID IT GO FAIRLY SMOOTH

YOUR LUCKY STARS
WILL SHINE ONE DAY
AND BRING YOUR DREAMS
ALONG THE WAY

Paul E Gray

HEARTBROKEN

DEATH IS A STRUGGLE
WHEN YOU LOSE SOMEONE YOU LOVE
YOUR EYES SEARCH THE HEAVENS
FOR HELP FROM UP ABOVE

EVERYWHERE I LOOK
I HAVE MEMORIES OF YOU
I'M SO LONELY
I DON'T KNOW WHAT TO DO

I GUESS YOU WOULD SAY
I'M A HEARTBROKEN MAN
TRYING TO GET BY
ANYWAY THAT, I CAN

YOU LIVE WITH SORROW
YOU LIVE WITH PAIN
YOU KNOW IN YOUR MIND
YOU WILL NEVER SEE YOUR LOVED ONE AGAIN

WHY DID YOU HAVE TO DIE
THEN LEAVE ME ALL ALONE
HOPING AND PRAYING
SOMEDAY YOU WOULD COME HOME

OLD AND LONELY
LOOKING FOR A FRIEND
HOPING TO MEET SOMEONE
BUT YOU DON'T KNOW WHEN

SOMEONE TO TREASURE

The Blue Collar Poet

TO LOVE WITH ALL YOUR HEART
PRAYING FOR SOMEONE
AND NEVER EVER PART

THE DAY WILL COME
WHEN I WILL DIE
I MIGHT BE MISSED
SOME MIGHT CRY

THE DAY IS CLOSE
I HOPE TO HIDE MY FEAR
I TRY TO SLEEP
I KNOW DEATH IS NEAR

I TRIED TO LIVE
A DECENT LIFE
SOMEWHAT KIND
SOMEWHAT NICE

Paul E Gray

SHORT AND SWEET

MY LIFE IS VERY STRESSFUL,
WHENEVER YOUR AWAY,
YOU KEEP ME WARM AND COZY,
EVERY SINGLE DAY.

I GO THROUGH THE DAY,
WITHOUT A CLUE,
WAITING FOR THE TIME,
THAT I COME HOME TO YOU.

I FIGHT DEPRESSION,
WHILE YOU ARE AWAY,
GO THROUGH THE HOURS,
WITH NOT MUCH TO SAY.

I KNOW IT'S SOMETHING YOU CAN'T CHANGE,
IT'S SOMETHING YOU MUST DO,
IT BREAKS MY HEART TO SEE YOU LEAVE,
I'M SO IN LOVE WITH YOU.

THE END

ONLY IF I COULD
TURN BACK THE HANDS OF TIME
I WOULD BE A BETTER PERSON
AND TRY TO EASE MY MIND

TRY TO CORRECT
ALL THE WRONGS I HAVE DONE
LIVE A BETTER LIFE
AND BE NICE TO EVERYONE

NOW THAT I AM OLDER
I NO LONGER WANT TO LIVE
I LOST MY BEAUTIFUL WIFE
I HAVE NOTHING MORE TO GIVE

ALL I HAVE ARE MEMORIES
SO I SIT HERE AND I PRAY
NOW I AM ALONE
WASTING TIME TO PASS THE DAY

I HAVE MADE MISTAKES
DONE THINGS I'M NOT PROUD OF
I'M ASKING FOR FORGIVENESS
AND HELP FROM UP ABOVE

I PRAY WITH ALL MY HEART
TO DO THE RIGHT THING
MAKE UP FOR MY MISTAKES
WHATEVER THE COST MAY BRING

NOW, I AM LONELY

Paul E Gray

ALONE WITHOUT A FRIEND
PATIENTLY WAITING FOR
MY BROKEN HEART TO MEND

I FEEL GUILTY
FOR SOME THINGS I HAVE DONE
SOMETIMES I WAS SELFISH
DIDN'T MEAN TO HURT ANYONE

REFLECTIONS

I KNOW THAT I AM MARRIED,
BUT FEEL SO ALL ALONE,
I DON'T BELIEVE SHE LOVES ME,
BY THE ACTIONS SHE HAS SHOWN.

THE WOMAN IS A DRINKER,
24 HOURS A DAY,
I HAVE TO GRANT HER WISHES,
AND WATCH THE THINGS I SAY.

THIS JUST MIGHT BE,
MY LAST WORDS OF WIT,
BEFORE I GIVE UP,
AND FINALLY, CALL IT QUITS,

I TRIED TO BE SO GENEROUS,
TO PEOPLE, OH, WHAT A JOKE,
NOW I SIT HERE WITH MY PROBLEMS,
NO HOPE NO FRIENDS I'M BROKE.

I THINK OF THEM QUITE OFTEN,
THE WOMEN I HAVE KNOWN,
BUT I NEVER REALLY THOUGHT,
SOMEDAY, I WOULD BE ALONE.
NOW I AM SO LONELY,
NO REASON LEFT TO LIVE,
I GAVE IT MY ALL,
I HAVE NOTHING LEFT TO GIVE.

I THINK OF MY LAST THOUGHTS,
NO SOLUTIONS LEFT IN SIGHT,

Paul E Gray

IT'S TIME TO CLOSE THE DOORS,
THEN TURN OFF ALL THE LIGHTS.

NOW I WAIT.

1/2/2021

DEATH

YOU JUST DON'T KNOW
JUST HOW YOU WILL DIE
WHO WILL CARE
WHO WILL CRY

SOME MIGHT BE HAPPY
SOME MIGHT BE SAD
IF LIFE'S BEEN CRUEL
PERHAPS YOU'LL BE GLAD

YOU MAY BE ALONE
AND NOT HAVE A FRIEND
YOU'RE ALL BY YOURSELF
YOU MIGHT WELCOME THE END

YOU MAY HAVE BEEN DEALT
ONE OF LIFE'S DIRTY BLOWS
OR IT MIGHT BE YOUR FAULT
FOR A LIFE THAT YOU CLOSE

YOU HAVE NO CHOICE
THE LAST BREATH THAT YOU TAKE
IT'S NOT UP TO YOU
IT'S LEFT UP TO FATE
IT WILL BE OVER
WHEN YOU TAKE YOUR LAST RIDE
IN AN AMBULANCE
WITH A MEDIC AT YOUR SIDE

I KNOW YOU'LL BE SCARED
WITH NOTHING TO SAY

YOU THINK TO YOURSELF

IS THIS MY LAST DAY

SORRY!

TEMPTATION

A RUSH CAME OVER MY BODY
THE NIGHT I TASTED YOUR WINE
AN EXPLOSION THAT ROCKED MY WORLD
I HOPED THAT YOU WERE MINE

THE DAY OUR EYES FIRST MET
YOU STOPPED MY BEATING HEART
FOR ME, YOU WERE HEAVEN SENT
I HOPED WE NEVER PART

THE BEAUTY OF YOUR BODY
THE SMILE ON YOUR FACE
I'M SUCH A LUCKY GUY
YOUR SKIN AS SOFT AS LACE

I CAN'T TELL YOU ENOUGH
ABOUT THE FEELINGS IN MY HEART
I KNOW IT FALLS TO PIECES
WHENEVER WE'RE APART

IT PROBABLY NEVER WAS MEANT TO BE
I'M SO FAR ALONG IN MY LIFE
YOU SURELY ARE SO BEAUTIFUL
TO YOUNG TO BE MY WIFE

MY JOURNEY IS ALMOST OVER
I DON'T KNOW HOW MUCH TIME I HAVE LEFT
SO, I JOT DOWN MY WORDS OF WISDOM
I'LL STRIVE TO DO MY BEST

AS I WAIT TO MEET MY MAKER

I'LL STRUGGLE AND PLOD ALONG
TRY TO KEEP MYSELF FOCUSED
UNTIL I'M CALLED TO TAKE ME HOME

LOSER

I HAD A PREMONITION
MANY YEARS AGO
KEPT IT TO MYSELF
NEVER TOLD A SOUL

AT FIRST, I COULD NOT BELIEVE IT
THOUGHT THIS WOULD NEVER COME TRUE
MIGHT SAY I MADE A BIG MISTAKE
MIGHT SAY I HAD NO CLUE

THINGS WOULD COME SO EASILY
I DIDN'T HAVE TO TRY
ALL MY FAME AND FORTUNE
I'M SUCH A LUCKY GUY

I DID NOT FOLLOW MY DREAMS
I WAS SOMEHOW LED ASTRAY
DIDN'T WANT TO WORK
I TOOK THE EASY WAY

IF I HAD ONLY KNOWN
THE PATH MY LIFE WOULD TAKE
I WOULD HAVE DONE THINGS DIFFERENTLY
FOR MYSELF AND HEAVENS SAKE

I'VE ALWAYS BEEN A PLEASER
TRIED TO HELP EVERYONE I CAN
PERHAPS A LITTLE MORE COURAGE
I MIGHT HAVE TAKEN A STAND

TO DO THE THINGS THAT ARE RIGHT

Paul E Gray

NOT THE THINGS THAT ARE WRONG
I WOULD HAVE TO STAY DILIGENT
I WOULD HAVE TO STAY STRONG

I THOUGHT I WOULD DO GOOD
IN EVERYTHING I TRIED
MY MIND PLAYED A TRICK ON ME
MY MIND HAS SOMEHOW LIED

SO, I GUESS I AM A LOSER
WITH ALL THE MISTAKES I'VE MADE
I CHOSE A LIFE OF CRIME
NOW IT'S TIME FOR ME TO PAY

EMOTIONAL JOURNEY

I DEDICATE

EMOTIONAL JOURNEY

TO MY WIFE

STEPHANIE M. O'SHAUGHNESSY-GRAY

AND MY SISTER-IN-LAW

CARLA GIUGNO

Paul E Gray

EMOTIONAL JOURNEY

I MISS YOU SO MUCH
I WEAR MY HEART ON MY SLEEVE
NEVER IN MY WILDEST DREAMS
DID I EVER THINK YOU'D LEAVE

YOU HAVE ALWAYS BEEN
HERE WITH ME
AT MY SIDE
FOR ALL MY WORLDLY NEEDS

TO GUIDE ME
TO HOLD ME
TO PRAISE ME
TO SCOLD ME

THERE'S NOTHING I CAN SAY
NOTHING I CAN DO
MY WORLD'S UPSIDE DOWN
BECAUSE OF THE LOSS OF YOU

SAVE A PLACE FOR ME IN HEAVEN
TO BE BY YOUR SIDE
LIKE THE DAY WE WERE MARRIED
AND I MADE YOU MY BRIDE
MY EMOTIONS RUN HIGH
WHEN I THINK OF YOU
I WOULD DO ANYTHING
JUST TO SAVE YOU

I TALK TO MYSELF
JUST TO HEAR MY VOICE

The Blue Collar Poet

SINCE YOU HAVE GONE
I HAVE NO CHOICE

I PATIENTLY WAIT
FOR MY DAY TO COME
WHEN WE WILL BE TOGETHER
JUST WHERE WE BELONG

Paul E Gray

FOLLOW YOUR HEART

FOLLOW YOUR HEART
FOLLOW YOUR DREAMS
IT MIGHT BE EASIER
THAN WHAT IT SEEMS

DON'T TURN YOUR BACK
ON WHERE YOU WANT TO GO
FOCUS ON THE FUTURE
TRY TO FOLLOW YOUR SOUL

FOLLOW YOUR DREAMS
FOLLOW YOUR HEART
IT'S LEFT UP TO FATE
WHERE YOU WILL START

THE PATH YOU TAKE
MIGHT SHOW YOU SOME FEAR
FOLLOW YOUR HEART
IT WILL BE PERFECTLY CLEAR

THE ROAD THAT YOU TAKE
WILL HAVE TWISTS AND TURNS
THE EXPERIENCE YOU SHARE
FROM THIS, YOU WILL LEARN

YOU HAVE A DESTINY
THAT YOU WILL FOLLOW
FOLLOW YOUR HEART
THERE'S ALWAYS TOMORROW

Paul E Gray

LONELINESS

LONELINESS IS MEAN
LONELINESS IS CRUEL
AWAKE EACH DAY
NOT KNOWING WHAT TO DO

YOU LOOK AROUND
FOR A FRIEND
BUT YOU'RE ALL ALONE
CAN'T SEEM TO MEND

NO ONE TO SPEAK TO
THE QUESTION IS WHY
YOU'RE ALL ALONE
NO ONE SAY'S HI

YOU HOPE EVERY DAY
FOR SOMEONE TO FIND
A PARTNER OR MATE
TO JUST EASE YOUR MIND

SOMEONE TO TALK TO
WHEN YOU'RE ALL ALONE
WHILE WAITING DESPERATELY
FOR SOMEONE TO PHONE

ONLY A FEW
KNOW WHAT I MEAN
THE PAIN IS ENORMOUS
YOU COULD JUST SCREAM

SO, YOU JUST LIVE
IN YOUR OWN LITTLE HELL

CAN'T THINK OF A THING
THAT MIGHT MAKE YOU WELL

NO ONE TO KISS
NO ONE TO HUG
NO ONE TO HOLD
NO ONE TO LOVE

LONELINESS CONSUMES YOU
IT'S DIFFICULT TO BREATH
YOU PRAY TO FIND SOMEONE
TO SATISFY YOUR NEEDS

ANOTHER DAY
HAS COME AND GONE
YOU'RE STILL ALONE
NO ONE'S COMING HOME
SO SAD
SO LONELY

SO HERE WE ARE AGAIN
EVERY POEM I WRITE
IS MORE DIFFICULT TO WRITE

Paul E Gray

ALONE

I AWAKE BACH MORNING
NOT KNOWING WHAT TO DO
ANOTHER EMPTY DAY
A DAY WITHOUT YOU

STEPHANIE WAS MY WIFE
ALSO MY BEST FRIEND
I'M WAITING FOR THE TIME
MY LONELY HEART WILL MEND

I FEEL GUILTY
FOR WHAT I COULD NOT DO
I FEEL GUILTY
FOR NOT SAVING YOU

NO ONE TO TALK TO
NO ONE TO TAKE CARE OF
NO ONE TO BE WITH
NO ONE TO LOVE

NO ONE TO TALK TO
NO ONE TO SEE
I SPEND MY DAYS
WATCHING T.V.

ALL I HAVE ARE MEMORIES
OF THE LIFE I ONCE KNEW
I SIT BY MYSELF
WITH NOTHING TO DO

I STARE AT MY PHONE
HOPING IT WILL RING

QUIETLY LISTEN
I DON'T HEAR A THING

NO ONE TO TALK TO
NO ONE TO SAY HI
THE SILENCE IS DEAFENING
MY QUESTION IS WHY

WAITING FOR MY HEART TO MEND
EVERYDAY MISSING YOU
HOW DO I EASE THE PAIN
I SURELY HAVE NO CLUE

I'M ALL ALONE
CAN'T UNDERSTAND WHY
WHILE WIPING AWAY
THE TEARS FROM MY EYES

I AWAKE EVERYDAY
REALIZE I'M ALONE
THINK ABOUT MY WIFE
WISHING SHE WOULD COME HOME

I CRY EVERYDAY
FOR MY WIFE, WHO'S NOT HERE
THE QUESTION OF WHY
IT IS NOT VERY CLEAR

I GO THROUGH THE MOTIONS
OF EVERYDAY LIFE
I WISH THINGS WOULD CHANGE
I MISS MY LOVING WIFE

Paul E Gray

I CRY EVERYDAY
WHAT AM I TO DO
I SPEND MOST OF MY TIME
THINKING OF YOU

THE TIME WILL COME
WHEN I'LL BE ALONE
I'LL TAKE THAT JOURNEY
ON MY OWN

WE ALL DIE
I KNOW THAT'S TRUE
I PRAY MY LAST THOUGHTS
WILL BE OF YOU

I LOVE YOU WEETIES

GOOD OR BAD

THE EYES TELL THE SECRETS
THAT OUR SOULS TRY TO HIDE
THEY KNOW THE TRUTH
THAT WE ALL KEEP INSIDE

HOPING NOT TO SHOW
YOUR UNPLEASANT PAST
THEY WILL NEVER GO AWAY
YOUR MEMORIES WILL LAST

YOU CAN GAZE INTO NOWHERE
SOMETHING LIKE A TRANCE
REFLECT ON YOUR MEMORIES
REFLECT ON YOUR PAST

HOPING YOU HAVE DONE THINGS
THE WAY THEY SHOULD BE
YOUR CONSCIENCE AND YOUR GUIDANCE
WILL TRULY HOLD THE KEY

LISTEN TO YOUR HEART
FOR THE THINGS THAT ARE REAL
YOUR SOUL IS TELLING YOU
EXACTLY HOW YOU FEEL
TRY TO BE GOOD
IN THE FUTURE THINGS YOU DO
YOU CAN CHANGE THE BAD
IT'S ALL UP TO YOU

IF YOU'VE BEEN GOOD
OR IF YOU'VE BEEN BAD

Paul E Gray

YOU'LL SEE THE TRUTH
BY THE LIFE YOU HAVE HAD

THE THINGS YOU DO
AND THE LIFE YOU LEAD
TELL YOUR STORY
IT'S YOUR LEGACY

CLOSET

I THINK ABOUT THE CLOSET
WHERE ALL MY SECRETS HIDE
I WONDER IF I'LL EVER FACE
THE TRUTH THAT LURKS INSIDE

SOME THINGS ARE VERY PAINFUL
THEY BRING ME MUCH DESPAIR
I CLOSE MY EYES TO FLUFF THEM OFF
PRETEND THAT THEY'RE NOT THERE

IT MUST BE KIND OF SCARY
TO WALK DOWN YOUR MEMORY HALLS
YOU KNOW ABOUT YOUR CLOSET
IT BEGAN WHEN YOU WERE SMALL

ALWAYS KEEP YOUR INSIGHT
YOUR HOPES AND DREAMS AND GOALS
KEEP YOUR DETERMINATION
NEVER LET IT GO

TURTLE DREAMS WILL KEEP YOU GOING
WHEN EVERYTHING SEEMS TO FAIL
WITH HARD WORK AND COMMITMENT
YOU'LL STAY ON THE RIGHT TRAIL

THE FORGOTTEN HERO

I WAS A SENIOR IN HIGH SCHOOL,
CAPTAIN OF THE FOOTBALL TEAM.
I GRADUATED IN JUNE,
IN AUGUST, I TURNED EIGHTEEN.

Paul E Gray

ON MY BIRTHDAY, I RECEIVED A NOTICE.
IT SAID I WAS A CHOSEN MAN,
TO FILL A GAP IN THE WAR MACHINE.,
IT WAS SIGNED BY UNCLE SAM.

SAID "GOODBYE" TO ALL MY FAMILY,
KISSED EVERYONE I LOVE,
I'M ON MY WAY TO BOOT CAMP
DON'T THEY REALIZE I'M A DOVE?

SO IT'S OFF TO FIGHT FOR MY COUNTRY,
DO MY MILITARY TOUR,
THEY SAY THEY WANT TO TRAIN ME,
FOR WHAT, I'M NOT EXACTLY SURE.

MY ARRIVAL WASN'T PLEASANT,
MASS CONFUSION EVERYWHERE.
WHATEVER HAPPENED TO MY CIVILIAN LIFE,
SOMEHOW IT DOESN'T SEEM FAIR.
BASIC TRAINING WASN'T EASY,
THE CERTIFICATE SAYS I'M A MAN,
I WAS TAUGHT THE ART OF KILLING,
WITH A WEAPON OR HAND TO HAND.

MY ORDERS ARE CUT IN ISSUED
I'LL BE SHIPPED TO A PLACE CALLED SAIGON
FROM THERE, I WILL GO TO THE DMZ,
BOY, IT'S A LONG WAY FROM HOME.

MY UNIT WENT INTO ACTION,
I WAS CAREFUL NOT TO LAG,
FOR I KNEW THAT ONLY ONE MISTAKE,
SENT ME HOME IN A BODY BAG.

The Blue Collar Poet

GUNFIRE WAS ALL AROUND ME,
MY BUDDIES DROPPED LIKE FLIES,
I WAS JUST DOING MY DUTY,
AND WAS NOT TO QUESTION "WHY"

IT HAPPENED IN THE JUNGLE
A DIFFERENT WORLD, A DIFFERENT TIME,
I MET "BOUNCING BETTY"
MY GOD, I STEPPED ON A MINE!

ME, I WAS WOUNDED,
OTHERS WENT INSANE,
BUT EVERYONE WAS MARKED,
WHO PLAYED THAT LOSING GAME.

FOR ME, THERE WERE NO BANNERS,
WHEN I RETURNED TO THE STATES
I WAS PUT IN A VA HOSPITAL
BEHIND THE WALLS AND LOCKED UP GATES.

AS THOUGH I WAS A CRIMINAL,
OR SOMETHING YOU TRY TO HIDE,
PLEASE DON'T BE ASHAMED OF ME,
AFTER ALL, I FOUGHT ON YOUR SIDE.

I WENT TO VIETNAM,
TO FIGHT A POLITICAL WAR,
I WENT TO VIETNAM,
TO FIGHT AN ENEMY I NEVER SAW.

NOW, I AM A DISABLED VET

Paul E Gray

WHAT AN "HONOR" TO BESTOW,
BUT SOCIETY WON'T ACKNOWLEDGE ME,
I AM THE FORGOTTEN HERO.

NOW THAT I AM OLDER

MY LIFE HAS BEEN A CHALLENGE
SOMETIMES, I THOUGHT I WAS CURSED
BUT IN TRUE REALITY
I GUESS IT COULD HAVE BEEN WORSE

NOW THAT I AM OLDER
IT SEEMS PERFECTLY CLEAR
THERE WILL COME A DAY
WHEN I WILL NO LONGER BE HERE

NOW THAT I AM OLDER
I'M SURE THERE IS NO DOUBT
LIFE HAS CHEWED ME UP
THEN HAS SPIT ME OUT

NOW THAT I AM OLDER
I AM A BEATEN MAN
I TRIED TO DO MY BEST
I TRIED TO TAKE A STAND

WHEN I TAKE MY LAST BREATH
I'LL BE SCARED THAT IS TRUE
IT'S A JOURNEY OF LIFE
WE ALL MUST GO THROUGH
I THINK OF DEATH
AND ALL THE PEOPLE I'VE KNOWN
THEY'RE NO LONGER WITH US
GOD HAS CALLED THEM ALL HOME

MY LIFE HAS NOW ENDED
IT'S TIME TO MOVE ON

Paul E Gray

AT MY FUNERAL
THEY'LL PLAY MY FAVORITE SONG

TODAY, I AM SILENT
I HAVE TO SAY I QUIT
YOU WILL NO LONGER HEAR
MY LOVELY WORDS OF WIT

NOW THAT IT IS OVER
I AM HOPING TO SEE
ALL THE FRIENDS AND FAMILY
WHO DIED BEFORE ME

REGRETS

I HAVE MADE MISTAKES
REGRETS, I HAVE A FEW
MY BIGGEST MISTAKE
WAS NOT MARRYING YOU

TO COMFORT YOU
TO HOLD YOU TO BE BY YOUR SIDE
TO KISS YOUR SWEET LIPS
AND MAKE YOU MY BRIDE

THE ONE WHO GOT AWAY
IT WAS NEVER MEANT TO BE
SO I SIT HERE WITH MY MEMORIES
AND WISH SHE HAD MARRIED ME

WE ALL HAVE HAD RELATIONSHIPS
SOME GOOD, SOME BAD
SOME MAKE YOU SMILE
OTHERS MAKE YOU SAD

SOME THAT GOT AWAY
MAY LEAVE YOU WITH REGRETS
OTHERS MAKE YOU HAPPY
HAPPY THAT YOU MET
I HAVE A SECRET HUNGER
FOR THE ONE WHO GOT AWAY
IF I COULD TURN BACK TIME
I WOULD GLADLY BEG HER TO STAY

THINK ABOUT YOUR PASSIONS
DECISIONS LEFT TO FATE

Paul E Gray

THE PEOPLE YOU HAVE LOVED
YOUR PERFECT SOUL MATE

THAT WOULD SURELY BE
A DREAM COME TRUE
IF YOU SAID YES
I WOULD MARRY YOU

I'VE WAITED SO LONG
TO BE IN YOUR ARMS
TO HOLD YOU SO CLOSE
AND KEEP YOU FROM HARM

I'VE WAITED SO LONG
TO SATISFY YOUR NEEDS
TO BE BY YOUR SIDE
ALWAYS TRYING TO PLEASE

HER NAME IS HELEN SOUZA
THE ONE THAT GOT AWAY
I WOULD SIMPLY DO ANYTHING
JUST TO HAVE HER STAY

I COULD NOT COMMIT
SHE CHOSE TO WALK AWAY
SHE LIVES IN WESTPORT
IT'S CALLED THE HEAD OF THE BAY

MY LIFE WOULD BE SO DIFFERENT
I COULD HAVE MADE SOME PLANS
NOW I AM SO LONELY
A BROKEN UNHAPPY MAN

I'M AFRAID TO LIVE IN THE FUTURE
FOR LIFE MOVES MUCH TO FAST
SO I SIT HERE WITH MY MEMORIES
AND CHOOSE TO LIVE IN THE PAST

WHEN MY LIFE IS OVER
AND I'M NO LONGER HERE
I HOPE TO SEE THE PEARLY GATES
AS I TRY TO HIDE MY FEAR

Paul E Gray

JUSTICE

WHO GIVES YOU THE POWER
TO OVERSEE AND GOVERN MY LIFE
YOU SIT THERE AND PROSECUTE ME
YOU DIDN'T LIVE WITH MY WIFE

YOU THINK YOUR HIGH AND MIGHTY
IN PARLIAMENT, MAYBE A LORD
IF YOU'D REVEAL YOUR INNER THOUGHTS
PERHAPS YOU THINK YOUR GOD

WHAT GIVES YOU THE RIGHT
TO SIT THERE ALL ALONE
HIGH UPON A PEDESTAL
LIKE A KING UPON HIS THRONE

LOOKING DOWN AT PEOPLE
WHO STAND AND AWAIT THEIR FATE
YOU THEN CHOOSE THE ONE YOU LIKE
THEN THE ONE YOU HATE

I REALLY DON'T BELIEVE
YOUR HONESTY IS REAL
POSSIBLY YOUR JUDGEMENT
IS JUST THE WAY YOU FEEL
OH, IF I COULD ONLY
TURN THE TABLES AROUND
I WOULD SIT ON THE PEDESTAL
YOU WOULD STAND ON THE GROUND

THEN AND ONLY THEN
YOU WOULD ACTUALLY SEE

The Blue Collar Poet

YOU HAVE NEVER BEEN
EXACTLY FAIR WITH ME

YOUR HATRED AND YOUR BIGOTRY
HAVE NOT GONE UNSHOWN
SHE HAS GOTTEN EVERYTHING
EVERYTHING I OWN

SHE WAS AWARDED THE CHILDREN
THE HOUSE AND THE NEWER CAR
TWO-THIRDS OF MY PAYCHECK
TO SQUANDER NEAR AND FAR

YOU SAY THAT YOU ARE ETHICAL
YOU SAY THAT YOU ARE FAIR
TO ONE, YOU SHOW YOUR ALLIANCE
ON THE OTHER YOU DON'T CARE

YOU THINK THAT YOU'RE SO RIGHTEOUS
THE EPITOME OF CLASS
BUT YOU'RE JUST A SUPERCILIOUS
IGNORANT, POMPOUS, ASS

Paul E Gray

DAD

I THINK AROUT MY FATHER
WHO HAS GONE BEFORE ME
I HOPE THAT HE IS PROUD
OF WHAT BECAME OF ME

I TRIED TO DO THE THINGS
THAT I WAS WORTHY OF
SHOWING A LITTLE KINDNESS
WITH MY HEART FULL OF LOVE

I HOPE THAT YOU ARE PROUD
OF WHAT I TRIED TO DO
FOLLOW IN YOUR FOOTSTEPS
AND DO WHAT YOU MIGHT DO

I'VE BEEN ALONE SINCE I WAS 7
WATCHED MY FATHER LEAVE TODAY
HE TOOK ALL HIS WORLDLY GOODS
LEFT IN A GRAY 51 CHEVROLET

TODAY MY WORLD CHANGES
IT LEAVES ME KIND OF SAD
HOW DO I GO ON
WITHOUT MY LOVING DAD

I TOLD MY MOTHER NOT TO WORRY
AS I TAPPED HER ON THE ARM
I WILL BE THE MAN OF THE HOUSE
I'LL KEEP EVERYONE FROM HARM

The Blue Collar Poet

I WAS SAD AND REALLY MISSED HIM
THERE WAS NOTHING I COULD DO
I WAS JUST 7 YEARS OLD
I GUESS I HAD NO CLUE

YOU TAUGHT ME TO BE BRAVE
YOU TAUGHT ME TO BE TRUE
YOU TAUGHT ME TO BE TUFF
I GET MY TENACITY FROM YOU

I HAVE NOT BEEN PERFECT
WITH SOME THINGS I HAVE DONE
I MADE MISTAKES
LIKE ANY HEADSTRONG SON

YOU TOLD ME TO BE STRONG
IF I WANTED TO SURVIVE
I FOLLOWED YOUR ADVICE
THAT'S WHY I AM STILL ALIVE

THANK YOU DAD
FOR ALL YOU HAVE TO DO
I AM A BETTER PERSON
ALL BECAUSE OF YOU, THANKS!

Paul E Gray

STEPHANIE

I THINK ABOUT MY WIFE
HER NAME WAS STEPHANIE
SHE HAS GONE TO HEAVEN
SHE IS NO LONGER WITH ME

SHE WAS MY WIFE
ALSO MY BEST FRIEND
I TRIED TO MAKE HER PROUD
RIGHT UP TO THE END

NOW, I MUST DEAL
WITH THE LIFE I ONCE KNEW
I AM SO LONELY
LONELY WITHOUT YOU

TRYING TO COPE
WITH EVERYDAY LIFE
I'M SO ALONE
I MISS MY BEAUTIFUL WIFE

SHE CHANGED MY LIFE
A DIRECTION I HAD NO CLUE
SHE OPENED DOORS
THAT I NEVER KNEW
MY MEMORIES STILL HAUNT ME
AND MAKE ME FEEL BLUE
I THINK OF MY WIFE
AND THE LIFE I ONCE KNEW

THE LIFE WE HAD
WHEN WE WERE ALONE

The Blue Collar Poet

THE LIFE WE HAD
WHEN WE WERE AT HOME

WE HAD A LIFE
WHERE DREAMS DID COME TRUE
WE HAD A LIFE
JUST ME AND YOU

WE WERE BLESSED WITH GOOD FORTUNE
MANY TIMES IN OUR LIVES
ESPECIALLY THE DAY
I MADE YOU MY WIFE

I CHERISH THE MEMORIES
OF THE LIFE I ONCE KNEW
I CHERISH THE MEMORIES
OF MY GREAT LIFE WITH YOU

THANK YOU
I WILL NEVER FORGET YOU
ALL MY LOVE UGLY

P.S.

I THINK THIS IS MY LAST POEM
MY POEMS BEGAN WITH YOU
SO I THINK MAYBE
THEY SHOULD END WITH YOU

IT SEEMS TO ME
AS IF I HAVE NOTHING MORE TO SAY
BUT WHO KNOWS,
MAYBE SOMEDAY THERE MAY BE MORE???

PAUL E. GRAY
THE BLUE-COLLAR POET

THIS IS A CONFESSION

TO PEOPLE WHO I OWE, TRYING TO MAKE AMENDS AND TRYING TO CLEAR MY SOUL. I TRIED TO TELL STORIES THAT MIMIC PARTS OF MY LIFE; SOME OF THEM WERE FUNNY, OTHERS CUT LIKE A KNIFE. IT'S OKAY; MY LIFE IS OVER. I KNOW IN HEAVEN I WILL SEE MY WIFE. I AM SO SORRY TO ACT THIS WAY, BUT I AM SO VERY LONELY. ONLY PEOPLE IN MY POSITION CAN RELATE TO HOW I FEEL. I HOPE SOMEHOW MY POETRY CAN EASE THE PAIN OF OTHERS. I'M ALL BY MYSELF; I'LL TRY TO CONTINUE ON WITH MY EVERYDAY LIFE, TRYING TO COPE WITHOUT MY BEAUTIFUL WIFE. MY WRITING TIME IS OVER; IT'S TIME FOR ME TO PAY FOR ALL MY LIFE'S CRUELTIES.

I HAVE NOTHING MORE TO SAY.
SORRY, PLEASE FORGIVE ME.

THANK YOU FOR YOUR TIME.

PAUL E. GRAY
DECEMBER 8TH, 2023.

P.S.

MY POEMS HAVE TO FEEL RIGHT
ACHIEVE A CERTAIN GOAL
ALWAYS TELL THE TRUTH
AND SATISFY MY SOUL

www.ingramcontent.com/pod-product-compliance
Lightning Source LLC
Chambersburg PA
CBHW041539120626
46551CB00019B/2770

* 9 7 8 1 9 6 5 4 0 8 1 2 4 *